Didn't We Have Fun!

paintings by

Hilda Robinson

story by

Hilda Robinson

&

Jeff Kunkel

CRICKHOLLOW BOOKS

Crickhollow Books is an imprint of Great Lakes Literary, LLC, of Milwaukee, Wisconsin, an independent press publishing quality fiction and nonfiction.

Our titles are available from your favorite bookstore or your favorite library jobber or wholesale vendor. For a complete catalog of all our titles or to place special orders, visit our website:

www.CrickhollowBooks.com

Didn't We Have Fun!
© 2012, Hilda Robinson and Jeff Kunkel

Publisher's Cataloging-In-Publication Data
(Prepared by The Donohue Group, Inc.)

Robinson, Hilda.
 Didn't we have fun! / paintings by Hilda Robinson ; story by Hilda Robinson & Jeff Kunkel. – 1st ed.

   p. : col. ill. ; cm.

   Summary: Hilda Robinson, artist and grandmother, shares the joys of growing up in a closely-knit African American family and neighborhood. She describes the games she played, the songs she sang, and chores she did long before television was invented.

   ISBN: 978-1-933987-17-0

   1. African Americans – Social life and customs – Juvenile literature. 2. Robinson, Hilda – Juvenile literature. 3. African American families – Pennsylvania – Philadelphia – Juvenile literature. 4. City and town life – Pennsylvania – Philadelphia – Juvenile literature. 5. African Americans – Social life and customs. 6. Robinson, Hilda. 7. Family life – Pennsylvania – Philadelphia. 8. City and town life – Pennsylvania – Philadelphia. I. Kunkel, Jeff, 1954– II. Title.

E185.86 .R63 2012
305.896/073/074811

First Edition

Printed in Canada

For my dear family,
for the wonderful staff of the Richmond Art Center,
and for all the lovely people of Jones Memorial United Methodist Church.
– Hilda Robinson

Contents

About Me

When I was four, Mama said to me, "Hilda, you're an artist." On my first day of kindergarten, she told my teacher, Mrs. Minkey, "Make sure you get my child an easel, paint, brushes, and paper." Mama also found me a drawing class at the Philadelphia Museum of Art. For that class we visited the zoo, and I made pencil drawings of animals and people.

In junior high school, one of my teachers, Mrs. Bea Claire Overton, said to me, "Hilda, you must try color!" She taught me how to create landscapes with crayons. Family and friends bought me beautiful paints and fine brushes and took me to art shows as far away as Washington, D.C.

When I was a grownup, I studied art at the University of California at Berkeley, graduating with my Master of Arts when I was almost fifty years old. Since then, my paintings have been displayed in art galleries, museums, offices, churches, and homes.

I paint with oil pastels, which are thick sticks of oil paint. I sit at my kitchen table, with music playing, and make a line drawing on a big sheet of green or red paper. Then I lay down one color after another, smudging and blending the colors.

I'm a grandmother now, but I still have many happy memories of being a child, and I love to paint these memories so that I can share them with other people – like you.

Hilda Robinson

The Six of Us

There were six of us then. Evelyn Florence, the eldest, was tall, dark, grand, and brilliant. She easily learned things like math, German, and piano.

Next there was Pearl Olivia – kind, serious, bookish, fair, and motherly. She played the violin.

Next there was me, Hilda Celestyne – dark, energetic, competitive, the tomboy, in love with art, music, and dance. I played the cello, sort of.

Ruth Erma was fair, pretty, smart, and obedient – the boys loved her! She played the piano and bass. The bass was bigger than she was, so to play it she had to stand on a riser.

Ruby Marcella, whom we called Bebe, was strong, fast, cute, and street-smart. She played the clarinet.

Archie Bernard, Jr., the only boy, was dark, happy, and spoiled, with lots of hair. He played the French horn, and he knew how to make money.

Ruby Marcella and Archie Junior were twins, born at the same time!

Most of us were born at home.

Mama and Daddy

My mother, Sarah Olivia Gray, was tall, strong, and beautiful. She held her head high and let everyone know that her children were the best!

We could always make her smile if we called her by her first name.

Mama cooked and cleaned for our family and other families. She also baked in the big ovens at the 292 American Legion Post.

My father's name was Archie Bernard Robinson. Daddy was short, dark, handsome, and slight, with a deep, bass voice.

He wore beautiful black suits, silk ties, and a Panama hat. He worked for the railroad and cooked for Valley Forge Military Academy, a popular school for rich boys from South America and Asia.

Daddy often answered our questions by saying, "Go ask your mother."

Whenever he had idle time, which wasn't very often, Daddy walked down to the barber shop and talked about baseball with the neighborhood men.

Home in Philly

We lived in Philadelphia, a big Pennsylvania city nicknamed *Philly*.

Philly is home of the Liberty Bell, Independence Hall,

and two hundred years of American history.

Our first home was close to Fairmount Park, on a street lined with red-brick row houses. Each house was home to a big family. In the summer, those houses got hot, so families spent a lot of time outside.

Children played on the front steps and sidewalks. Grownups sat in wooden rocking chairs on the front porches and kept an eye on the children.

Everyone went "Ooo!" and "Ahh!" when a cool breeze came along.

We had no television in our home – they weren't invented yet – but we did have a big, floor radio. In the afternoon, we listened to

Tony and the Pirates and *Jack Armstrong, All-American Boy.*

In the evening, our whole family listened to music and entertainment shows like

Texaco Opera and *Major Bowes Original Amateur Hour.*

The six of us also listened to spooky shows like *The Green Hornet* and *The Shadow,*

and good guy-bad guy shows like

The Lone Ranger and Zorro.

Reading

We also loved to read, so each week we brought home books from the public library. If each of us borrowed one book, we had six books to share at home!

We adored fairy tales like *The Grimm Brothers' Tales* and *The Wizard of Oz,* mysteries like the *Bobbsey Twins,* and poetry by Byron, Shelley, Keats, and Paul Laurence Dunbar, the first nationally known African-American poet.

Dunbar wrote in two different kinds of English – the English of the classical poets and the English of the black community.

My favorite poem of his, "In the Morning," begins like this:

> *'LIAS! 'Lias! Bless de Lawd!*
> *Don' you know de day's erbroad?*
> *Ef you don' git up, you scamp,*
> *Dey'll be trouble in dis camp.*

Homework

At home, the six of us did lots of schoolwork,

like arithmetic, spelling, and reading.

The older ones taught the younger ones to read even before they got to school and helped one another spell long words and memorize the multiplication tables.

We studied together at the dining room table, but in winter, we sat at the bottom of the stairs – right above the gush of warm air from the floor furnace grate.

Visitors

We liked to sit at the top of the stairs or behind a couch and eavesdrop on the grownups.

They spoke about politics, religion, and sports - especially about Joe Louis, a black boxer who became heavyweight champion of the world. When Joe Louis fought, each family on our street gathered in their living room and listened to the fight on their floor radio.

If Louis won, everyone ran outside, shouting and laughing, and the boys pulled white sticks of chalk out of their pockets and wrote on the sidewalk:

JOE LOUIS, WORLD CHAMP

Saturdays

On Saturdays, Mama did the laundry, and we helped. Using a stick, we pushed the heavy, wet clothes into the wringer. The rollers flattened each piece of clothing and squished out the water, which smelled of bleach ammonia and Rinso Soap. Then we helped Mama hang the laundry on our backyard clothes lines. The wind and sun dried our clothes and made them smell clean and fresh.

Afterwards, we walked to the Joy Movie House to watch movies like *Snow White* and *Sleeping Beauty,* and movies with child-star Shirley Temple. Movies cost fifteen cents.

All Dressed Up

Most of the time, my sisters and I wore white dresses, with matching bows in our hair and brightly-colored bows tied to our waist. We wore white leather shoes on regular days, and black patent-leather shoes for special occasions.

On the Saturday before Easter, Christmas, and other holidays, Mama took us girls to the beauty parlor. Mrs. Johnson, the hairdresser, heated our curls until they went limp and our hair became straight! Mrs. Johnson chewed wax, which I thought was great!

23

Cuddling

We spent a lot of time at

home up under the grownups,

where we

cuddled,

giggled,

read,

and napped.

We loved to sit in Mama's

lap and fall asleep.

Asleep

Sometimes Mama was so
tired from all her work that she fell
asleep, too.

School

We walked to school each day, even if it was raining or snowing. Daddy carried the younger ones in his arms during real bad weather, and Philadelphia had plenty of that – hurricanes, blizzards, downpours, windstorms, and floods!

In the classroom, we practiced Reading, Writing, and Arithmetic. We memorized dates and names from American History.

We also kept an eye on what happened outside. We watched fat, lazy clouds drift by in the sky, trees sway in the wind, and snowflakes twirl and tumble to the ground.

And of course, I watched boys.

We watched the rain come and go too, and when the rain was over, we went outside and it smelled like rose petals and Lux soap!

At recess, we played song and clap games, like Step Back, Sally, and Here We Go, Zudio, and Patty Cake, Patty Cake.

We also played games like Marbles and Pick Up Sticks. Double Dutch was a game of jump rope, with two ropes.

We played Hopscotch, too, and Baby In the Air, a running game.

More Fun & Games

We also played on slides, monkey bars, and merry-go-rounds,

but we especially loved the swings.

We would swing way up high and then jump out, fall through the air,

and land on our feet with a thud and a grunt.

Boys

The boys played games like stickball and basketball.

In stickball, a broom handle or mop pole was used as a bat, and a baseball was cut in half and used as the ball.

The half-ball was pitched so it dropped and curved. It took a good batter to hit a half-ball!

When the
boys wanted to
play basketball,
they found a bas-
ket, and knocked
out the bottom.

Then one
boy got on the
shoulders of an-
other and nailed
the basket to a
telephone pole or
wall.

Sides were
picked. First team
to twenty-two
won. This was
no complaints, no
crying, no fouls,
let's-get-down
basketball!

Rollerskating

Not far away, there was a steep street we called Sulzberger Hill.

This hill meant danger and fun!

In summer, we took our rollerskates and skated down Sulzberger Hill.

Each of us held onto a long rope

and played Crack the Whip all the way down.

Oh, what speed!

When we fell, we scraped and bruised our knees and elbows,

but that didn't stop us!

In winter, we slid down Sulzberger Hill

on sleds or pieces of thick cardboard.

The Park

We liked to walk to Fairmount Park, one of the largest city parks in America.

The park had tall trees, green lawns, ponds, paths,

and water which bubbled to the surface from an underground spring.

Mama often gave us gallon jugs and sent us to the park.

There, we filled the jugs with clear, cold spring water

and carried the water home.

Water is heavy, but we were happy to help Mama.

We also picked dandelion greens in the park, and for dinner,

Mama cooked the greens with salt pork,

with white lima beans and biscuits on the side.

Yum!

A Family Picnic

Once in a while, my aunts and uncles came from Maryland or Virginia,

and we had a picnic.

We played games like Potato Sack Race.

The men sat in the shade and played cards and checkers.

The women set out plates of

fried chicken,

potato salad,

watermelon, and pitchers of iced tea,

with sweet potato pie, cake, and vanilla ice cream.

We made the ice cream in hand-cranked freezers filled with cream, and surrounded
with coarse salt, all covered with a white cloth.

Sundays

On Sundays, Mama got up extra early and baked, and we got dressed in our Sunday clothes.

Evelyn, Pearl, Ruth, Ruby, and I wore pink, baby blue, or yellow summer coats, with matching hats, and black, patent-leather shoes.

When it got cold, we wore extra coats and muffs.

Since Ruby and Archie Junior were twins, they often wore matching clothes.

When Mama's butter-shined yeast rolls and loaves of bread were browned and crusty, she took them out of the oven, put them in waxed paper, and sent us out to deliver them to her customers.

Some of her customers lived ten blocks away, so we did a lot of walking on Sunday mornings!

Mr. Hebron, our music teacher, was supposed to get a dozen rolls each Sunday, but he rarely got a full dozen because we always ate one or two before we got to his house.

Church

Later on Sunday mornings, we walked to White Rock or Monumental Baptist Church and attended Sunday worship. The women wore red, white, and yellow dresses, with matching shoes and hats, and lots of face powder and perfume.

The
men wore
dark suits
and silky
ties.

The
ushers wore
uniforms
with white
gloves.

The
choir wore
neck-to-
ankle white
robes.

Singing

We sang so many hymns that we learned every verse by heart! Sometimes, we sang duets for the adults during tea time.

In the afternoon, we went across the street to Reeves Memorial Presbyterian Church for more prayer and singing.

Each summer, we attended the Vacation Bible School at Reeves, where we memorized long bible passages, verses like "work out your own salvation with fear and trembling for it is God who works in you to will and to do of his good pleasure."

Our worship was colorful, loud, and busy.

We got to our feet, prayed, clapped and counter-clapped, sang and hummed.

The preachers shouted, and we answered "Well?" or "Take your time!" or "Amen!"

Sometimes, one of the women got extra happy and shouted and waved her arms so much that an usher had to calm her.

We sang all kinds of music at church. We sang Negro spirituals like "Deep River" and "Swing Low, Sweet Chariot" and "Steal Away," and hymns like "Just As I Am" – the song I sang when I joined the church at age eleven.

Didn't We Have Fun!

We didn't have a car.

We didn't have a television.

We didn't have much money.

But we had parents who loved us,

a good home,

plenty to eat,

and lots of books, games, and friends.

Best of all, we had

each other.

Acknowledgements

Courtesy Dana Davis Photography

Thanks to the following individuals and organizations whose paintings by Hilda Robinson are included in this book:

Richmond Art Center
Dr. Bill Hoskins
Malia Bishop
Rae Louise Hayward
Marci Jenkins
Jeff Kunkel and Mary Elyn Bahlert
Reginald and Kimberly Hill
Wanna Wright
Etta Lundy
Henri Schuyers and Melba Lazenby-Jenkins
Dr. Ramona Bishop

Additional paintings in this book are from the collection of the artist.

Special thanks to Emily Anderson of the Richmond Art Center of Richmond, California, for her wonderful help in providing digital files of a number of Hilda's paintings for this project.

HILDA ROBINSON lives and paints in Oakland, California. Her artistic talents were first nurtured at the young age of three when her father presented Hilda with her first box of paints. As a young adult, she studied painting at the Tyler School of Fine Arts at Temple University, and completed her BA and MA studies in art at UC–Berkeley.

Robinson has received the prestigious Jan Hart-Schuyers Merit Award through the "Art of Living Black" exhibitions at Richmond Art Center, as well as the Atlanta Life Insurance Purchase Award.

Robinson's colorful and playful oil pastels are based in everyday glimpses of African Americans at play and leisure, at home, at school, and at church. Her art is deeply rooted in African-American traditions of celebration, storytelling, and humor, with a glowing transcendence that embraces the joys of life found in families and communities everywhere.

JEFF KUNKEL grew up in a Wisconsin family of fine story-tellers – farmers, teachers, preachers, factory workers, and merchants. He received his Master of Divinity Degree from Garrett-Evangelical Seminary in Evanston, Illinois. At mid-life, he studied drawing and painting at the California College of the Arts in Oakland, California.

He is now an artist, an ordained United Methodist pastor, and an accomplished writer. Jeff has authored two collections of short stories, two books about Alaska history, and four picture books for kids, one of which was awarded Best Theological Book of the Year for children.

He lives with his wife in an old house on a hill in Oakland, not far from Hilda Robinson.

Jeff and Hilda have collaborated on many projects in public schools, churches, and art galleries. This is their first picture book together.